2/22/10

ENVIRONMENTAL FOOTPRINTS

How Big Is Your Energy Footprint?

Paul Mason

Marshall Cavendish
Benchmark
New York

Louisburg Library
Bringing People and Information Together

This edition first published in 2010 in the United States of America by Marshall Cavendish Benchmark.

Marshall Cavendish Benchmark
99 White Plains Road
Tarrytown, NY 10591
www.marshallcavendish.us

All Internet sites were available and accurate when sent to press.

First published in 2008 by
MACMILLAN EDUCATION AUSTRALIA PTY LTD
15–19 Claremont Street, South Yarra 3141

Visit our website at www.macmillan.com.au or go directly to www.macmillanlibrary.com.au

Associated companies and representatives throughout the world.

Copyright © Paul Mason 2008

Library of Congress Cataloging-in-Publication Data

Mason, Paul.
  How big is your energy footprint? / by Paul Mason.
  p. cm. – (Environmental footprints)
  Includes index.
  ISBN 978-0-7614-4411-4
  1. Renewable energy sources–Environmental aspects–Juvenile literature. 2. Power resources–Environmental aspects–Juvenile literature. 3. Energy development–Environmental aspects–Juvenile literature. 4. Renewable energy sources–Environmental aspects–Case studies–Juvenile literature. 5. Power resources–Environmental aspects–Case studies–Juvenile literature. 6. Energy development–Environmental aspects–Case studies–Juvenile literature. I. Title.
  TJ808.2.M37 2009
  333.79–dc22

                                                                    2008048107

Edited by Anna Fern
Text and cover design by Cristina Neri, Canary Graphic Design
Page layout by Domenic Lauricella
Photo research by Legend Images
Illustrations by Nives Porcellato and Andrew Craig

Printed in the United States

Acknowledgments
The author and the publisher are grateful to the following for permission to reproduce copyright material:

Front cover photograph: Earth from space © Jan Rysavy/iStockphoto; coloured footprint © Rich Harris/iStockphoto. Images repeated throughout title.

Photos courtesy of:
AAP/AFP/Abdelhak Senna, **23**; AAP/AP Photo/Thomas Herbert, **16**; AAP Image/Solar Systems, **21**; City of Melbourne, **27**; © Joss/Dreamstime.com, **6**; altrendo images/Getty Images, **24**; © AVTG/iStockphoto, **7**; © Rob Broek/iStockphoto, **13**; © william casey/iStockphoto, **19**; © Oleksandr Gumerov/iStockphoto, **8**; © Peter Engelsted Jonasen/iStockphoto, **22**; © Magali Parise/iStockphoto, **29**; © Terraxplorer/iStockphoto, **5**; © Paul Tessier/iStockphoto, **26**; © manuel velasco/iStockphoto, **14**; © Mark Weiss/iStockphoto, **3** (top right), **30**; Rob Cruse Photography, **10**; © Thomas Barrat/Shutterstock, **18**; © luchschen/Shutterstock, **12**; © Losevsky Pavel/Shutterstock, **9** (bottom); © Otmar Smit/Shutterstock, **20**; © Lee Torrens/Shutterstock, **28**; © Holger W./Shutterstock, **11**.

Please note
At the time of printing, the Internet addresses appearing in this book were correct. Owing to the dynamic nature of the Internet, however, we cannot guarantee that all these addresses will remain correct.

1 3 5 6 4 2

Contents

Environmental Footprints   4

The Energy Industry   6

Energy Sources   10

Case Study **Energy from Earth**   13

Energy Production   14

Case Study **Chernobyl Nuclear Disaster**   17

Case Study **Carnarvon Solar-Energy Farm**   21

Energy Use   22

Case Study **Carbon Offsetting**   23

Case Study **Ground-Source Heat Pumps**   25

Case Study **Council House 2**   27

How Big Is Your Energy Footprint?   28

Future Energy Footprints   30

Glossary   31

Index   32

Glossary Words
When a word is printed in **bold**,
you can look up its meaning in the
Glossary on page 31.

Environmental Footprints

This book is about the footprints people leave behind them. But these are special footprints. They are the footprints people leave on the **environment**.

Heavy Footprints

Some people leave heavy, long-lasting footprints. They do this by:

⊕ acting in ways that harm the environment

⊕ using up lots of **natural resources**, including water, land, and energy

It can be hundreds of years before the environment recovers from heavy footprints.

Light Footprints

Other people leave light, short-lived footprints. They do this by:

⊕ behaving in ways that harm the environment as little as possible

⊕ using the smallest amount of natural resources they can

The environment recovers from light footprints much more quickly.

As the world's population grows, more natural resources will be needed. It will be important not to waste resources if we are to leave light footprints.

The world's population is expected to continue growing in the future.

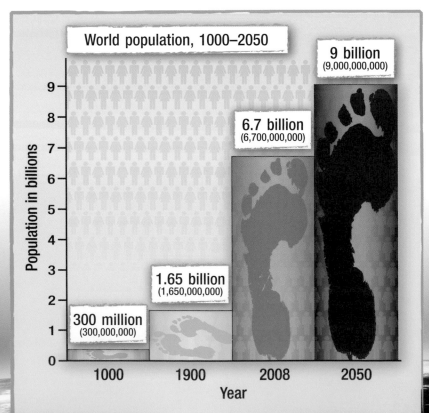

World population, 1000–2050

9 billion
(9,000,000,000)

6.7 billion
(6,700,000,000)

1.65 billion
(1,650,000,000)

300 million
(300,000,000)

Population in billions

1000   1900   2008   2050

Year

Leaving on lights in office buildings when they are not needed wastes electricity and leaves a heavy energy footprint.

What Makes Up an Energy Footprint?

An energy footprint is made up of the effects of energy use on the environment. This includes the amount of energy people use to power things such as lights, cars, or televisions. It also includes the energy used to make the goods people buy, and the energy used to grow food.

A lot of energy is produced in ways that badly damage the environment. People who use a lot of this energy have heavy energy footprints. Using less energy, and energy produced in less damaging ways, leaves behind a lighter footprint.

What sort of energy footsteps are you taking? Read on to find out!

The Energy Industry

Energy is used to light people's homes, power their cars, grow food, and make goods for people to buy. Over the last 200 years or so, a giant industry has grown around the world to provide this energy.

Where Energy Comes From

Traditionally, people have gotten most of their energy from burning things. At first, this meant burning wood for heat or light. Today, though, much of the world's energy comes from burning **fossil fuels**.

Fossil fuels include coal, petroleum oil, and natural gas. People use energy from fossil fuels in various ways. They use gasoline to power their cars, for example, or use electricity made by burning coal to light their homes.

Fossil fuels are burned at power stations to make the energy we need in our everyday lives.

Alternative Energy Sources

Alternative energy sources to fossil fuels include the Sun's energy, the power of flowing water, wind power, and the heat energy contained inside Earth. These are all used in different parts of the world to produce energy, often in the form of electricity.

Nuclear Power

Another alternative to fossil fuels is nuclear power. Nuclear power is produced using **uranium**. Scientists use the uranium to produce tremendous amounts of heat, which is then used to make electricity. The world's largest reserves of uranium are in Australia, although none of Australia's energy is produced using nuclear power.

Nuclear power stations use water for cooling, so they are often near lakes or the sea.

Having plenty of energy allows us to enjoy useful appliances, such as refrigerators.

Benefits of the Energy Industry

Many of the benefits people enjoy as part of modern daily life are a result of having affordable, plentiful energy. These benefits include:

⊕ being able to keep homes comfortably warm or cool

⊕ having light available when it is dark outside

⊕ being able to travel over long distances quickly, by car, bus, train, or airplane

⊕ enjoying the products of modern industry, including toys, cars, and computers

Almost every aspect of our daily life depends on the energy industry.

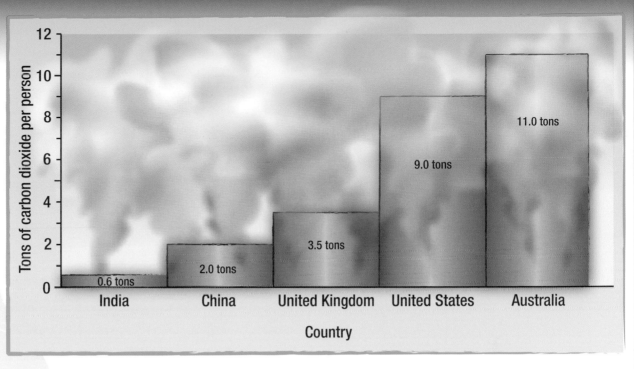

This graph shows how much carbon dioxide was released into the atmosphere per person in different countries in 2007.

Tons of carbon dioxide per person

- India: 0.6 tons
- China: 2.0 tons
- United Kingdom: 3.5 tons
- United States: 9.0 tons
- Australia: 11.0 tons

Country

Environmental Costs of the Energy Industry

All the convenience of modern life comes with environmental costs.

- Burning large amounts of fossil fuels releases **carbon dioxide**, which has a damaging effect on Earth's **atmosphere**.
- **Pollution** from burning fossil fuels can damage the health of living things.
- Damage to wildlife and the landscape is caused by **oil spills**.
- **Contamination** after leaks from nuclear power stations causes deaths and poisons the land for years to come.

Almost all cars release carbon dioxide pollution when their engines are running.

These costs leave behind a heavy energy footprint that will last for hundreds of years.

Energy Sources

Energy sources are the raw materials from which people get energy. The type of energy sources people use affects the size of their energy footprint.

Fossil Fuels

Fossil fuels are used to create most of the world's energy. They are made from the remains of plants and animals that died millions of years ago. These remains sank down under Earth's surface. Over time, they turned into fossil fuels, either solid coal, liquid oil, or natural gas. Each of these can be burned to create usable energy.

Rethink!

Battery-powered flashlights use up energy resources. Wind-up flashlights are better for the environment because they are powered by human energy.

This wind-up flashlight is powered by hand so it has a small energy footprint.

Extracting Fossil Fuels

Fossil fuels have to be **extracted** from Earth before they can be used to create usable energy. The mining process leaves a heavy footprint on the environment in several ways.

⊕ **Opencast mines**, where coal is dug out, scar the landscape. Pollution from the mines can poison nearby water supplies and soil. This affects the local plants and animals.

⊕ Mining coal releases methane, a harmful **greenhouse gas**.

⊕ Extracting and transporting oil can lead to oil leaks. The oil poisons local water supplies and soil. Fish and plants become coated in oil and die. Some experts say that the effects of a major oil spill can last more than ten years.

Fossil Fuels Running Out

The amount of fossil fuels left in Earth is getting smaller. Once it has all been extracted, there will be no more.

Opencast coalmines can scar the landscape.

Clean Energy Sources

Clean energy sources cause little or no harm to the environment. They leave a far lighter energy footprint than fossil fuels. Many clean energy sources can be found in nature. They include the power of the wind, moving water, and the Sun.

Every day, a huge amount of solar energy falls on Earth. Converting sunlight into usable energy makes it unnecessary to burn fossil fuels. It is also possible to get usable energy from wind, flowing rivers, waves, and Earth itself.

Solar panels provide this apartment complex with electricity.

Choosing to use clean energy will give you a lighter energy footprint.

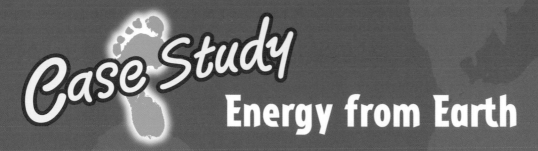

Case Study
Energy from Earth

Iceland lies over an area where volcanic activity occurs close to the surface of Earth. The people of Iceland have used heat energy from this volcanic activity since about 1930. Heat energy from Earth is called geothermal energy.

To collect geothermal energy, pipes are drilled down into the ground and filled with water. The water heats up underground and is then pumped up to the surface. The water then heats 95 percent of city buildings and supplies hot water for bathing.

Geothermal energy also provides Iceland with electricity. Heat from Earth is used to drive **turbines**, which produce electricity. Iceland also uses the power of flowing water to make electricity. All of Iceland's electrical power comes from these sources, which means Iceland has one of the lightest energy footprints of any country.

Swimmers enjoy the warm water that fills lakes beside one of Iceland's many geothermal power stations.

Energy Production

Producing energy damages the environment. How much it damages the environment depends on how the energy is produced. This determines the heaviness of the energy footprint.

Fossil-Fuel Power Stations

Fossil-fuel power stations can burn oil and gas to produce electrical energy, but most burn coal. The heat produced from burning fossil fuel is used to create steam, which drives turbines. These turbines create electrical energy that can be used by homes and industries.

However, burning fossil fuels is linked to **global warming**, the biggest threat to the environment today. Global warming is the increase in Earth's average temperature.

Using the off switch instead of standby cuts an electrical appliance's energy use.

14

Global Warming

Global warming is happening right now. As Earth's temperatures rise, **deserts** spread, rainfall becomes less predictable, and sea levels get higher as polar ice melts. The world's weather may become more extreme, with more **droughts**, **hurricanes**, floods, and other disasters.

Causes of Global Warming

Almost all scientists agree that people contribute to global warming. One of the ways they are doing so is by burning fossil fuels. This releases greenhouse gases, which trap heat within Earth's atmosphere. Fossil-fuel power stations burn vast amounts of fuel each day. The energy they produce has a heavy energy footprint.

Greenhouse gases, especially carbon dioxide, are released when fossil fuels are burned and help to increase global warming.

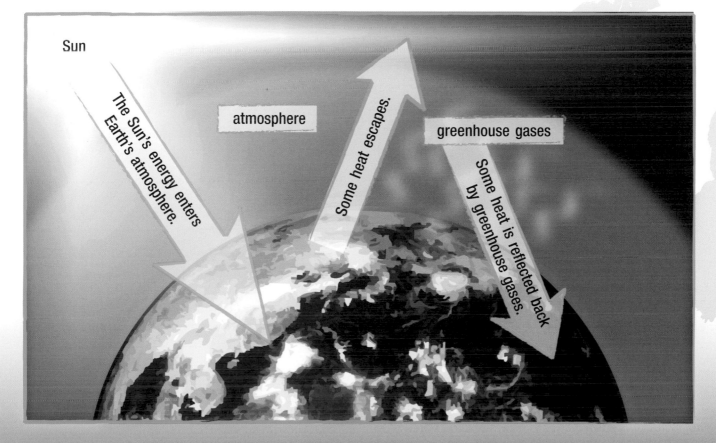

Sun

The Sun's energy enters Earth's atmosphere.

atmosphere

Some heat escapes.

greenhouse gases

Some heat is reflected back by greenhouse gases.

Nuclear Power Stations

Nuclear power stations are an alternative to fossil-fuel power stations because generating nuclear power does not produce greenhouse gases. Nuclear power can affect the environment in other ways, however. It can have an extremely heavy environmental footprint.

Radiation Leaks

Nuclear power stations produce radiation, which is harmful to living things. Radiation is usually very carefully contained within a power station, but it sometimes leaks out. When this happens, it can affect the environment for thousands of miles and many years.

Nuclear Waste

Waste material from nuclear power stations releases radiation for hundreds of years. Unless this waste is sealed away, the radiation leaks out and poisons the environment.

Nuclear waste is so dangerous that it has to be transported in special containers.

Case Study
Chernobyl Nuclear Disaster

On Saturday, April 26, 1986, the world's worst nuclear disaster happened at Chernobyl in Ukraine. An explosion at the Chernobyl nuclear power plant shot **radioactive material** high into the sky. The material was then blown by the wind.

By Monday, April 28, the radioactive waste had spread as far away as Sweden. It would eventually spread over thousands of miles.

As a result of the accident:

- large areas of land could no longer be used to grow crops or raise animals
- rivers were poisoned
- between 4,000 and 93,000 people are eventually expected to die because of radiation

Between 5 and 8 million people still live in areas affected by the disaster. The long-term effects on their health are not yet known.

The Chernobyl disaster affected most of Europe. People close to the site of the accident were exposed to more than 100 times the normal rate of radiation.

Multiples of normal rates of radiation

- No detectable rise
- .001–1
- 1–5
- 5–10
- 10–20
- 20–40
- 40–100
- 100+

Hydroelectric Power

Hydroelectric power is produced by flowing water. Usually, water from a dam pours through an opening, driving a turbine. The turbine produces electricity.

Hydroelectric power does not produce greenhouse gases, but it affects the environment in other ways. When a dam is first built, for example, the land behind it is flooded. People, plants, and animals lose their homes. Despite this, many people argue that hydroelectric energy has a far lighter footprint than fossil-fuel energy.

Biomass Energy

Biomass energy comes from plants. The biomass is burned to provide heat, in the same way as fossil fuels are burned. Burning biomass releases the same amount of carbon dioxide that the plants removed from the atmosphere while growing.

The Three Gorges Dam hydroelectric project in China generates electricity from the power of moving water.

Rethink!

When plants grow, they take in carbon dioxide from the air. Planting trees is a good way to reduce the amount of harmful greenhouse gases in the atmosphere.

Wind turbines are often grouped together in wind farms.

Power from the Sea

Waves and tides wash against most of the world's coasts. Several ways to use the movement of the sea to generate electricity have been invented. In the future, this could become an important light-footprint source of energy.

Geothermal Energy

Geothermal energy comes from the heat within Earth. It can be used to produce both hot water and electricity.

Wind Power

Wind power can be used to produce energy. The wind turns propellers on giant wind turbines. The turbines make electricity. No greenhouse gases are released once the turbines are built, so wind-power energy has a very light energy footprint. Around the world, twelve times as much wind-power electricity was produced in 2007 as in 1997.

Solar Power

Solar power is energy that comes from the Sun. It can be used to heat water and produce electricity for homes and businesses. In places where the Sun shines a lot, solar farms have been set up to harvest the Sun's energy. Once the farms have been set up, they have a very light energy footprint.

Small-Scale Energy Production

Wind and solar power can both be used to produce energy on a small scale. People can put solar panels on the roof of their house, or they can use a small wind turbine or hydropower device to generate electricity. This gives them a very light energy footprint. In many countries, it is possible for small-scale energy producers to sell any leftover electricity to the power companies.

These solar panels will help the home owner save money on electricity bills, as well as have a light energy footprint.

Choosing to use energy whose production is less harmful to the environment, such as biomass energy, hydroelectricity, geothermal, solar, and wind power will give you a lighter energy footprint.

Case Study
Carnarvon Solar-Energy Farm

In October 2005, a solar-energy farm opened in the town of Carnarvon, in Western Australia. Carnarvon was chosen partly because it is one of the areas in the world that gets the most light from the Sun.

The farm started relatively small, with just 144 solar panels. Even so, in its first year the farm produced enough energy to supply Carnarvon with power for four days.

It would have taken about 2,200 gallons (10,000 liters) of fuel oil to produce a similar amount of energy.

Solar energy produces no greenhouse gases, so electricity from Carnarvon solar-energy farm has a light energy footprint.

The solar panels at a solar energy farm are lined up so that they catch as much of the Sun's energy as possible.

Energy Use

People use energy for many things in their daily lives. How they use it has a big effect on their energy footprint. Using energy when you do not need it creates a heavier footprint. Saving energy creates a lighter one.

Travel

Transportation is one of the main sources of carbon dioxide, a greenhouse gas that is one of the causes of global warming. Cars and most buses, trucks, and airplanes get their energy by burning fossil fuels. Trains run on electricity, which is also usually produced by burning fossil fuels.

Rethink!

Traveling on foot or by bicycle instead of in a car reduces the size of people's energy footprints.

Special lanes for cyclists, such as this road in Berlin, Germany, make it safer to travel by bike.

Case Study
Carbon Offsetting

Carbon offsetting is a way for people to try to make up for the carbon dioxide gas released by burning fossil fuels. It first became popular as a way of making up for traveling by airplane, which burns large amounts of fossil fuel.

Carbon offsetting works by planting trees, because trees use carbon dioxide to grow. The original idea was that paying for trees to be planted would use up the carbon dioxide that had been released.

Today, carbon-offset organizations offer other ways to make up for carbon dioxide pollution such as:

⊕ buying solar panels for people in poorer countries, so that they will not need to burn fossil fuels for light

⊕ paying for small hydroelectric power stations to be built in poorer countries, so that electricity will not have to come from burning fossil fuels

These offer alternative ways to fill in the energy footprint left behind by burning fossil fuels.

Solar panels installed on this house in Morocco through a carbon-offsetting scheme produce enough electricity to power four to eight lightbulbs.

23

Energy at Home

In wealthy countries, energy used at home produces a quarter of the carbon dioxide that is released by energy use. Saving energy at home can make a person's energy footprint much lighter.

Heating and Cooling

Controlling the temperature inside homes uses up a lot of energy. Boilers usually burn gas to heat water for radiators. Putting on extra clothing instead of turning up the heat saves energy and results in a lighter footprint.

Air conditioning for cooling runs on electricity. Wearing loose, cool clothes and using cold drinks to cool down instead of having the air conditioner on saves energy.

Turning down the temperature control on the heating and putting on a warm sweater saves a lot of energy.

Ground-Source Heat Pumps

Ground-source heat pumps are an alternative to heating and cooling systems that use fossil fuels. Not far below Earth's surface, the ground stays at a steady temperature. This enables ground-source heat pumps to warm or cool buildings.

A pipe is sunk down into the ground. Water is pumped through the pipe and back to the surface.

If the building above is cold, the water is warm in comparison and warms the building up. If the building is hotter than the ground, the water carries some of this heat underground, where it is **absorbed**.

If the water is pumped through the system using solar or hydroelectric energy, ground-source heat pumps have a very light energy footprint.

Heating and cooling a house with a ground-source heat pump produces a lot less carbon dioxide than other heating and cooling systems that use fossil fuels.

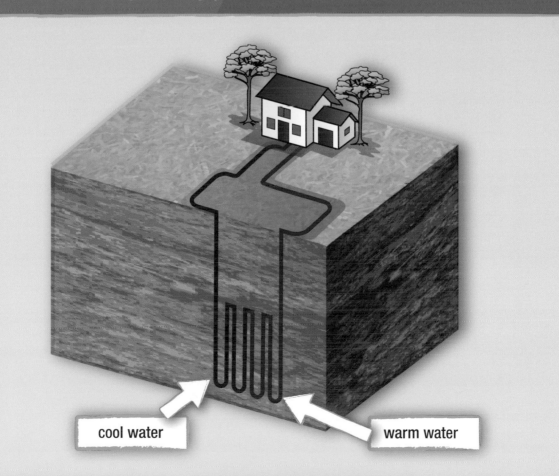

cool water

warm water

Lightbulbs

Lightbulbs run on electricity. They only use small amounts, but lots of small amounts add up. Many people today use low-energy lightbulbs and make sure they turn off lights in rooms when they leave them.

Electronic Devices

Electronic devices use electrical energy. The more devices people use, the heavier their energy footprints. It is possible to save energy by:

- unplugging devices such as DVD players, televisions, and computers when they are not being used
- never using the standby button
- only using devices such as washing machines, dishwashers, and tumble dryers when they are full

Saving energy in these ways will lighten your energy footprint.

Houses that use low-energy lightbulbs reduce their power bills and have smaller energy footprints.

Choosing to take simple steps to use less energy in your everyday life will give you a lighter energy footprint.

Case Study
Council House 2

Council House 2, also known as CH_2, in Melbourne, is Australia's most environmentally friendly office building. It is filled with features designed to lighten CH_2's energy footprint.

- The computer screens need only 50 percent as much energy as normal.

- Low-energy lights use only 35 percent as much energy as normal.

- The north side is shielded from the Sun's heat by a "vertical garden" of vines.

- Inside, CH_2 is heated or cooled using the Sun's energy and water and wind turbines.

- Sixty percent of the building's hot water comes from solar panels on the roof.

CH_2 is far better for the environment than the office building it replaced. It uses 15 percent of the electricity, 13 percent of the gas and 28 percent of the water used by the previous building. It also produces only 13 percent of the greenhouse gases.

CH_2 is a ten-story office building in Melbourne, Australia.

27

How Big Is Your Energy Footprint?

The size of a person's energy footprint depends on how the energy they use was made, and how much they use. How big do you think your footprint is?

Where Does Your Energy Come From?

Energy from sources that do little or no harm to the environment has a light footprint. Producing light-footprint energy does not release greenhouse gases into the atmosphere. Solar energy, wind energy, water power, and geothermal energy are all "clean" energy sources.

Nuclear energy produces no carbon dioxide, but there are major safety concerns about nuclear accidents and nuclear waste.

Burning fossil fuels to release their energy releases greenhouse gases. These are the main cause of global warming. Using energy from fossil fuels makes your energy footprint heavier.

How big do you think your energy footprint is?

Wind power is a source of "clean" energy.

Rethink!
Electricity companies now supply at least some of their energy from green energy sources. This is produced in ways that are less harmful to the environment.

Work Out Your Energy Footprint!

Ask yourself how often ("never," "sometimes," or "often") you do these things:

- ⊕ travel by bicycle or walk
- ⊕ travel by ship or train rather than by airplane
- ⊕ have a cold drink instead of turning on the air conditioning
- ⊕ get up to turn off the television or DVD player instead of using standby
- ⊕ turn off the computer instead of letting it sleep

Walking or riding a bike instead of asking your parents to drive you are easy ways to reduce your energy footprint.

If your answers are mostly "never," you have a heavy energy footprint. If you mostly answered "sometimes," your footprints are average. If you gave a lot of "often" answers, you are leaving only light environmental footprints.

Future Energy Footprints

You can choose to take light footsteps or heavy footsteps. If people continue leaving heavy footprints, it could affect the environment for thousands of years to come.

What You Can Do

The Internet is a great way to find out more about what you can do to take lighter footsteps. Try visiting these websites:

🌐 **http://www.carbonfund.org**
   This site contains lots of advice on how to reduce the size of your greenhouse-gas footprint.

🌐 **http://www.carboncounter.org/about-offsets/what-is-an-offset.aspx**
   Here you can find out how carbon offsets help to fill in your environmental footprint from using a lot of fossil-fuel energy.

🌐 **http://managemyemissions.com/carbonCalculator.php**
   This site has a carbon calculator, where you can work out how big your environmental footprint is at home, through motor travel, through air travel, and through public transportation.

Some of the search terms you might use to find information about energy and the environment include:

- 🌐 coal-fired power stations, pollution
- 🌐 geothermal energy, Iceland, and New Zealand
- 🌐 energy, carbon calculator.

What will YOU do to change your energy footprint in the future?

Glossary

absorbed
soaked up or taken in

atmosphere
the layer of gases that surrounds Earth, enabling humans, animals, plants, and other creatures to survive

carbon dioxide
a gas that is used by plants to help them grow, and that is released when fossil fuels are burned

contamination
making something impure or dirty by introducing harmful or poisonous material

desert
area with very little water, where only certain plants and animals can live

droughts
periods of time without enough rainfall, when water becomes scarce, crops fail, and plants and animals suffer or die

environment
the natural world, including plants, animals, land, rivers, and seas

extracted
taken out or removed

fossil fuels
the remains of plants and animals from millions of years ago, which have been buried deep under Earth's surface and there turned into coal, oil, and gas

global warming
process by which Earth's average temperature is getting warmer

greenhouse gas
gas that contributes to global warming, which is often released when fossil fuels are burned

hurricanes
violent storms with very high winds, capable of damaging buildings, trees, and anything in the way

natural resources
natural substances, such as wood, metal, coal, or water, that can be used by humans

oil spills
accidental leaks of petroleum oil into the natural environment

opencast mines
giant pits dug at the surface of the ground in order to get out coal or other minerals

pollution
damaging substances, especially chemicals or waste products, that harm the environment

radioactive material
a substance that releases a stream of tiny particles that, in all but the smallest doses, are poisonous to most living things

solar power
power from the Sun, which can be turned into electricity by solar panels

turbines
machines in which moving fluid or gas, such as water or steam, rushes through and forces propeller blades to spin, which can be used to make electricity

uranium
a poisonous mineral that affects the health of plants and animals when it breaks down

Index

A

air conditioning, 24
air travel, 23, 29
alternative energy sources, 7,
    12, 16, 18–21

B

biomass energy, 18
building design, 27

C

carbon dioxide, 9, 15, 18, 22,
    23, 24, 28
carbon offsetting, 23, 30
Carnarvon (Western Australia)
    solar-energy farm, 21
cars, 5, 6, 9
Chernobyl disaster, 17
clean energy sources, 12,
    18–21, 28
coal, 6, 10, 11, 14
cooling homes, 8, 24, 25
Council House 2 (CH$_2$) building,
    Melbourne (Australia), 27
cycling, 22

D

developing countries, 23
droughts, 15

E

electrical appliances, 14, 26
energy footprint, 5, 28–29
energy consumption, 6, 8, 22,
    24, 26
environmental footprints, 4

F

fossil-fuel power stations,
    14–15
fossil fuels, 6, 9, 10–11, 15, 22,
    28

G

geothermal energy, 13, 19
global warming, 14–15, 22, 28
greenhouse gases, 9, 11, 15, 16,
    18, 19, 22, 24, 28
ground-source heat pumps, 25

H

heating homes, 8, 24, 25
hurricanes, 15
hydroelectric power, 12, 18,
    20, 23

I

Iceland, 13

L

lightbulbs, 26

M

methane, 11
mining, 11

N

natural resources, 4
nonrenewable resources, 11
nuclear accidents, 9, 16, 17
nuclear power, 7, 16, 28
nuclear waste, 16

O

oil spills, 9, 11

P

pollution, 9, 11, 23
population growth, 4
power stations, 14–21

R

radiation, 16, 17

S

small-scale energy
    production, 20
solar power, 12, 20, 21, 23

T

Three Gorges Dam hydroelectric
    project, China, 18
transportation, 22

U

uranium, 7

W

walking, 22
wave power, 19
wind power, 12, 19, 20
wind-up electric devices, 10